How a seed grows into sunflower

Written by
David Stewart

Illustrated by
Carolyn Franklin

Hold the page
to the light
see the
flower opening.

BOOK HOUSE

Published in Great Britain in 2009 by
Book House, an imprint of
The Salariya Book Company Ltd
25 Marlborough Place, Brighton BN1 1UB

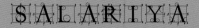

HB ISBN 978-1-905087-25-9
PB ISBN 978-1-905087-26-6

Visit our website at **www.book-house.co.uk**
or go to **www.salariya.com** for free electronic versions of:
You Wouldn't Want to be an Egyptian Mummy!
You Wouldn't Want to be a Roman Gladiator!
Avoid Joining Shackleton's Polar Expedition!
Avoid Sailing on a 19th-Century Whaling Ship!

Author: **David Stewart** has written many non-fiction
books for children on historical topics, including *You Wouldn't
Want to be an Egyptian Mummy!* and *Avoid Sailing on the
Titanic!* He lives in Brighton, England, with his wife and son.

Artist: **Carolyn Franklin** is a graduate of Brighton
College of Art, England, specialising in design and
illustration. She has worked in animation, advertising and
children's fiction and non-fiction. She has a particular interest
in natural history and has written many books on the subject
including *Life in the Wetlands* in the WHAT ON EARTH? series
and *Egg to Owl* in the CYCLES OF LIFE series.

Consultant: **Monica Hughes** is an experienced
Educational Advisor and author of more than one hundred
books for young children. She has been Headteacher of a First
School, Primary Advisory Teacher and Senior Lecturer in Early
Childhood Education.

A catalogue record for this book is available
from the British Library.

Printed in China.

PAPER FROM
SUSTAINABLE
FORESTS

Contents

flower-head

petal

bumblebee

What is a sunflower?

A sunflower is a plant that lives for only one year. It is very tall, with a long, thick stem, and has a single, large, yellow or orange flower-head. A sunflower plant needs lots of sun and water to help it grow.

stem

ladybird

stem ————

Plants use energy
from the sun to
make food.

What is a seed?

Inside a sunflower seed there is a new plant in miniature and a store of food. The hard outside of the seed is called a **seed-coat**. During the cold winter months the seed lies buried in the ground.

Soil contains **minerals**. These are special foods that help the plant to grow.

worm

seed-coat

The warm spring sun and rain make the seeds start to grow. This is called **germination**.

seed

Hold the page up to the light to see the seed germinating.

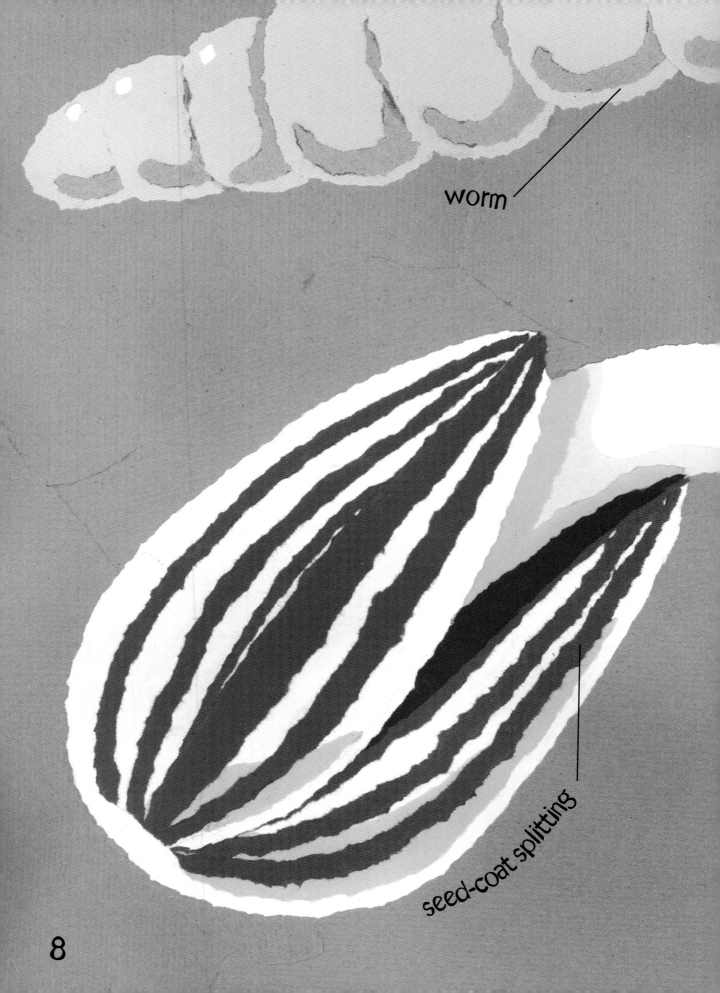

worm

seed-coat splitting

8

What happens in the spring?

When the soil warms up in the spring, the hard seed-coat splits open. The first root pushes its way out and then grows down into the soil. Soon afterwards a shoot will sprout. The shoot will lift up the seed-coat as it grows upwards out of the soil.

root _____

soil

What do roots do?

Small roots now sprout from this first root. They take in minerals and water from the soil to feed the plant. Once the shoot has pushed up through the soil, it grows two tiny green leaves called **seed-leaves**.

ladybird

seed-coat

seed-leaf

bud

shoot

The store of food inside the seed helps the plant to grow. The bud, hidden between the seed-leaves, pushes the seed-coat away.

small roots

rain

Why do sunflowers need rain?

As the young sunflower plant grows taller, more leaves sprout. The leaves use air, rainwater and energy from sunlight to make food for the plant. This process is called **photosynthesis**.

ladybird

roots

leaf

stem

garden snail

Flower buds form and
the roots grow longer.
The roots reach deep
down to take water from
the soil. They also help to
hold the sunflower steady.

sunlight

sunlight

How tall do sunflowers grow?

I t takes about 13 weeks for a sunflower to grow fully. Some sunflower plants can grow up to more than 3 metres tall. The main root can reach 3 metres down below the ground!

Plants make their own food.
The leaves take in sunlight
and moisture from the air.
Then they make sugars that
feed the plant.

ladybird

What *is* a flower bud?

At the top of the stem there is a flower bud. The flower bud follows the sun all day. When the plant is nearly fully-grown, the flower bud will open. There is a flower-head inside the flower bud.

leaf

ladybird

It is the flower's job to **reproduce**. It makes new plants that will grow next year.

flower-head

flower bud

stem

ladybird

17

How big is the flower-head?

The flower-head is larger than a dinner plate. Big yellow petals surround it, making it even bigger. During the day, its petals open up. At night, its petals fold in and close.

The big, round flower-head is made up of lots of tiny flowers. Each tiny flower will become a new sunflower seed.

yellow petal

leaf

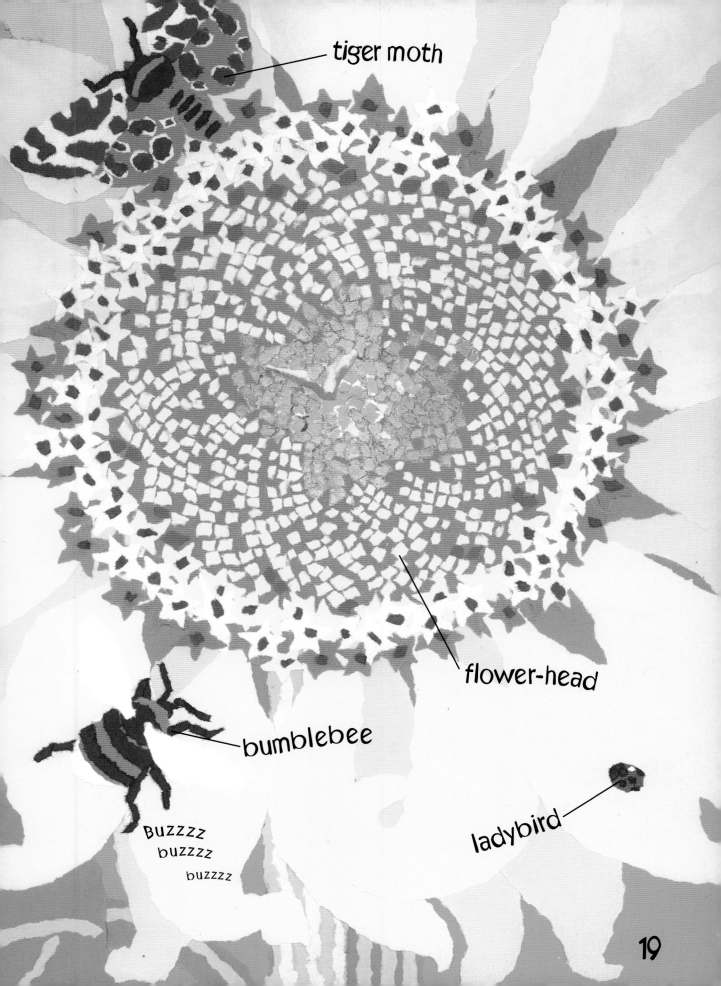

tiger moth

flower-head

bumblebee

Buzzzz
buzzzz
buzzzz

ladybird

19

Buzzzz buzzz

honey-bee

Buzzzz

pollen grains

pollen sac

Why do sunflowers need insects?

There is **nectar** inside the sunflower head. Bees and other insects visit the plant to drink the nectar. There is also **pollen** on the sunflower head. The bees pick up the sticky pollen grains. As the bees fly from one plant to another, they move the pollen from plant to plant. This is called **pollination**. Sunflowers need pollen to produce new seeds.

Buzzzz
buzzzz

honey-bee

Buzzzz
buzzzz

ladybird

Bees need pollen for food. Some
bees collect pollen on their hairy
bodies. Other bees put it into yellow
bags on their legs called pollen sacs.

flower-head

seeds

ladybird

How are seeds carried far away?

Birds peck at the tiny seeds in the flower-head as they ripen. Some seeds are eaten and some are blown away by the wind.

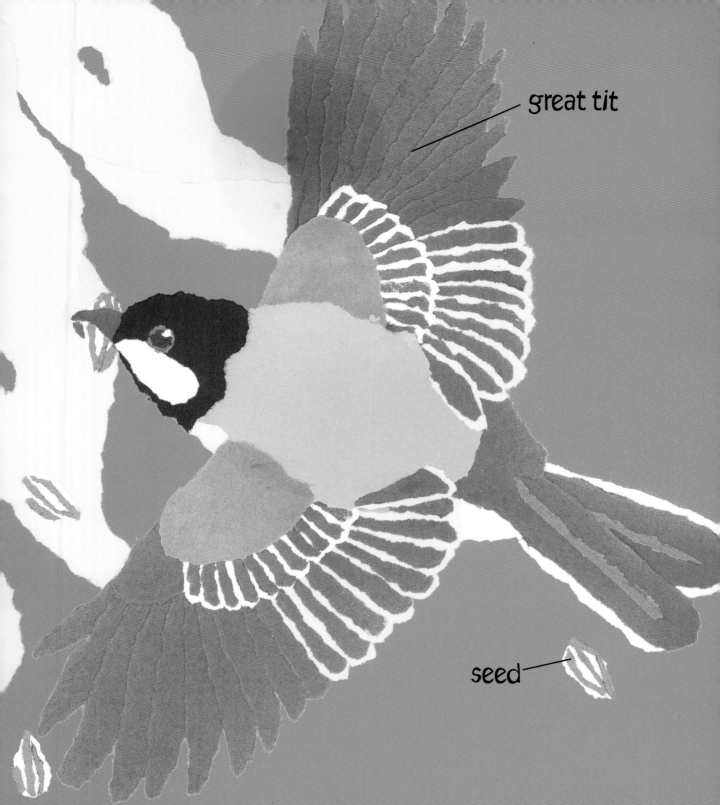

great tit

seed

Seeds on the ground can stick to the fur of a passing animal. These seeds may fall off far away from the main plant.

23

What happens in the autumn?

In autumn the sunflower dies. The seeds that have not been eaten or carried away fall to the ground. Many of the seeds will grow into new sunflower plants in the spring.

ladybird

tree sparrow

seed

The birds eat some of the
sunflower seeds. They also
scatter some of the seeds so
that new plants can grow.
This is good for both the birds
and the plants.

Sunflower facts

Sunflower seeds are about one centimetre long.

A sunflower head can grow to be as wide as 40 centimetres across.

The main leaves of a sunflower are heart-shaped. They are about 20 centimetres wide and 30 centimetres long.

Sunflowers were originally grown by Native Americans.

Most sunflowers are grown in North and South America, but they also grow in Europe.

budding

9 weeks

spring

5 weeks

the seed sprouts leaves

seed

Sunflower seeds were brought from America to Spain in 1510.

About 200 years ago farmers started to crush the seeds to make sunflower oil.

Sunflower oil is used for cooking. The seeds are good to eat, too.

The leftovers of the crushed seeds are used as animal food.

summer

autumn

12 weeks

flowering

fully grown

withering

falling seeds

Things to do

Grow your own sunflower

You will need:
One empty yoghurt pot
Edible sunflower seeds
Strips of card
Pencil
Garden soil

1   Fill the yoghurt pot with soil.

2   Make a hole in the soil with your finger (about 3 cm deep) and drop in one seed.

3   Cover the seed with soil. Put in a card strip with the date written on it.

4   Stand the pot in a sunny spot and water well. Be careful not to let the soil get too dry — or too wet.

5   When your plant has at least four leaves, move it carefully into a patch of soil outside.

6   Measure the height of your sunflower every week as it grows.

7   Keep a notebook to record how your sunflower is growing.

My Diary

Date: 6th

The seed-leaves grow

Date: 7th

The plant is 3 cm tall, and its two leaves are 1.5 cm long.

new seed
ready to
grow

birds spread
seeds

root starts
to grow

Life cycle of
a sunflower

shoot starts
to grow

seeds
fall

leaves
appear

flower-head
appears

flower buds
appear

30

Things to do

Find out if a sunflower turns towards the sun

You will need:
One sunflower plant
   (before the petals
   have opened)
A sunny day
A clock or watch

Record the sun's position at different times of the day.

Note which way your sunflower is facing each time.

Words to remember

Germination The first stage of growth, when the seed begins to sprout.

Minerals Substances in the soil that help plants grow.

Nectar A sweet juice that plants produce to attract insects.

Photosynthesis The process plants use to make energy from sunlight.

Pollen A powder produced by plants, which the plants use to help make new seeds.

Pollination Moving pollen from one plant to another so that seeds can grow.

Reproduce To make new plants.

Seed-leaves The first leaves that are already in the seed when it sprouts.

Index